ANTHOLOGY OF FAITH

Sayantan Datta

PARTRIDGE

Print information available on the last page.

To order additional copies of this book, contact
Partridge India
000 800 919 0634 (Call Free)
+91 000 80091 90634 (Outside India)
orders.india@partridgepublishing.com

www.partridgepublishing.com/india

CONTENTS

MY POETRY

I write of blue, red and green, sometimes of yellow and grey,
Sometimes I write of fields and mountains, and sometimes dried rivers, instead.
Some days I write of battles and wars, other days, of the duels of my mind,
All shades, and hues, and corners and caves, you will find in the rhymes I penned.

A while back, inspired by a man in a coat, walking down the road by my window pane,
I wrote of a journey of no end or gain, a path of tears and pain.
The man in the dark coat, in my dreams, came to laugh the next night,
And, I wrote of mysterious joys I felt, in laughing for no reason instead.

Yesterday, I went walking in the forest, I saw a bird fly flutter astray;
Filled me with sorrow, today, I wrote, all life must fly away.
I never know, today or tomorrow, what emotion so strong, shall be born,
To inspire from mine echoing heart, a memorable rhyme and song.

A MILE AWAY

So many miles I have walked past,
Open fields, past dense and towering forests,
Past the marketplace ferrying fruits, flowers and faith,
Past the gardens, crimson and red,
My destination seems but a mile away.

Who is this voice humming away?
This is not your path, I hear it say.

I run past children, playing in the park,
And their mothers, looking out, smiling and pretty,
Past the chimneys pouring industry into the air,
And engines humming with purpose.
My destination seems but a mile away.

Who is this voice humming away?
This is not you path, I hear it say.

I amble by a temple gate, the preachers, the saint,
Past the humble man, kneeling in humble praise,
Past an orchard in bloom, past a silent loom,
Past a family feasting on their milk and bread.
My destination seems but a mile away.

Who is this voice that hums away?
This is not your path, I hear it say.

I stop to look ahead and back,
Back at a feeble distant candlelight, and ahead,
The mile ahead beckons with purpose, yet,
Every step forward seems leaden with weight.
My destination seems but a mile away.

This is not my path, this is not my path,
Who is this voice, in chorus now, chants and prays?

Is it not my path to these rewards, is it not my fate?
Is it not my crown that lies beyond these boulders up ahead?
My heart and mind lament different songs, and
True love in a feeble candlelight calls.
My destination still but a mile away.

This is not my path, this is not my path,
Who is this voice, from the roads passed by, that calls?

THE LETTER OF MY FAITH

Show to me your letter of faith,
That shows me the man you are.

Show me the letter of your birth,
That proves your intrinsic worth.

Show me the letter of your God,
That tells me of the colour of your blood.

Show me the letter of your colour,
That shows me the grain you're worth.

Show me the letter of your land,
That proves the price of your life.

Show me the letter of your past,
That tells me the path chosen for your tomorrow.

Show me the letter of my faith,
That proves to me my worth.

WHERE ARE YOU

I answered your call to action,
When your faith called for battle,
When your sermon was of war,
I walked on fire, "fire won't burn, fire shall purge."
I left behind all who defied, behind in the crowd,
And now I am alone, directionless in the dark.
Where are you?

I felled men, and women and a child,
When you said they defied your faith,
I bled them dry, "blood needed to flow,"
I burned and tore through the crowd, in search of promised paradise.
I left my love standing by a distant stream,
And now I am alone and directionless in the dark.
Where are you?

I built this palace with riches of plunder,
When you promised me glory in loot,
And you preached "beauty was vice,"
I slaughtered my way to you, "true faith lay in plunder and sacrifice".
I turned away from all, that I held dear, to be who you wanted me
to be,
And now I am alone and directionless in the dark.
Where are you?

I forced your faith on the weak and poor,
When you told me that was ordained,
And you told me that was faith,
I made men slaves to your word, you said your sermon was supreme,
I slay along the way, the helpless and the kind, memories that haunt
my mind
And now I am alone and directionless in the dark.
Where are you?

I shrunk to a lesser man,
When you needed me to be small,
When you needed my sacrifice off all,
I gave back all my riches, my heart, my soul, to that you proclaimed holy.
Never looking back, never, to breathe or smile, stopping my stride,
And now I am alone and directionless in the dark.
Where are you?

LET YOU BE YOU, LET ME BE ME

Let you be you for a little while,
Let me be me for a little while,
A little unfinished and a little bit jagged,
A little unrefined and a little bit ragged,
Before we dive back to the dulled tones of life,
And disappear in the flow.

Let you dream free for a fleeting moment,
Let me dream free for a fleeting moment,
Of flying through the clouds, away from this noise,
In a colour of the skies, of our choice,
Before we wake up to the everyday mime,
Trapped in the shackles of time.

Let you soar high for a passing day,
Let me soar high for a passing day,
Going beyond where imagination loses its way,
Where the winds blow free and angels dream,
Before we fall to the dusty ground again,
Cast to a destined and dull end.

I FOUND A BOOK OF PAINTINGS

I found a book of paintings, buried deep in my new attic,
Through layers of dust and age peeked a jacket, now worn and ragged;
No one knew from whence it came or who had, in it, spoken with paint,
No one knew of the faces in the once bold strokes, now faded, and
faint.

Therein I found, a painting of a young child in the arms of a dying
widow,
Grief and innocence, and helpless eyes;
The widow had greys of wretched ages, etched over her faded smile,
Expressionless amid humble walls, under grieving skies.

There was a painting, made only in shades of grey,
A street corner I've not seen the likes of before,
An unkept head of hair, a tattered tent, and a feeble streetlight,
Under a starless and moonless night, it made a dim sight.

Someplace near the centre of the folds,
I saw a painting of a couple, how in love they seem!
Bathing in the setting sun, a weathered shore of meandering streams,
Waiting for the tide of promised hope, a tide of joyful dreams.

Thereafter follow, a few violent sketches and strokes,
Reeking of dark and pain, in abstract strokes and flows,
A disturbed yet strong mind, lay dissected on a canvas,
Pouring out it's pain, memories, and shapeless faith.

There then are a series made of bright and abundant colours,
The couple again, in the throes of love,
In the midst of grandeur, and friends, and wealth,
Joy in their mirth, although a strange loneliness in their eyes.

This book of paintings that I found in my new home,
Abruptly ends, a lonely pyre, by an abundant river shore,
A poem half written, and half a dream,
Half a myth, half a tale, and just a half told folklore.

GOD, WHO BE WORTH MY FAITH

They tell me to believe in a God,
A God all potent, and all seeing,
And yet an almighty who stands aloof,
To man's gravest sins.

They tell me to believe in a God,
A God preached with dark text on white pages of faith,
That was meant to enact an ungodly path,
To preach of divide and hate.

They tell me to believe in a God,
A God that hasn't tolerance of the stray,
Designed to punish and berate,
The voice of dissent and those who cry 'nay'.

They tell me to believe in a God,
A God who ne'er to me, speaks,
I only hear your words of faith, words that by the powerful spread
Words of vengeful and painful deeds.

Where be the God of the miracle of birth
And the God who blessed the miracle of earth,
Where lies hidden the God who showered rain and sun,
Find me my God who be, worth my faith.

I AM SORRY

What reparations can I make but say that I am sorry,
For not speaking when I should have screamed,
For bowing when I should have protested,
For not looking back when I should have run to see.

What amends can I make but say that I am sorry,
For looking away when I should have seen,
For being silent when I should have joined in song,
For not being where I should have been.

What change can I make but say that I am sorry,
For my hands in my pockets when they should have attended your pain,
For not believing when I should have had faith,
For closing my eyes when I should, a soldier, have been.

What atonement would be just but say I am sorry,
For not writing when poetry of fire I should have spewed,
For lying subdued when you called to brandish my arms,
For pretending to be lost when, a beacon of hope, I should have been.

THE BATTLES WE WON
AND LOST TO YOU

The rise and fall of the phantoms of our past,
Have driven home this realization, at last,
For all we've lost and found, and lost again,
We never have let off the pain.

The morning sun, the evening winds blow,
And the stars, their halo about the lunar glow,
Blinking witnesses to our battles, we won and lost to you,
Our revolts, and our anguish, our lives burnt through.

Futile has been this pursuit of a promised stake,
Destined to bow and bend, and break,
Deep in our hearts we always knew,
Never shall we receive the doers due.

The hours and days and years gone by,
Below the grassy fields, layers of dried mud and blood,
Bears witness to the battles we won and lost to you,
Our revolt, and our anguish, our lives burning through.

Betrayed and broke, decimated souls,
Cursed for life to your will, our heads hang low,
Fallen, and yet, we must rise and walk again,
To feed fuel to the fire that must burn.

The fortunes of the feeder, the chained fate of those fed,
The crown of the executioner, and the wounds of the dead
Are witness to this battle we won and lost to you,
Our revolt, and our anguish, our lives burning through.

THE WORST OF IT ALL

You die for your love,
And you kill for your hate,
And you stand up for what you believe,
And you fight to the death.
The worst of it all is that here, in the future someday
No one shall move or be swayed,
And you'd die, and kill, and stand tall and fight,
For all that you'd do, you'd be forgotten, all in vain

You could holler and scream,
And cry foul at all things obscene,
Wrong and evil,
And must be done away with.
The worst of it all is that here, in the future someday
No one will have listen or changed,
The burns of your heart and the wrinkles of your pain
For all that you have said shall be forgotten, all in vain.

You could write a poem or tell a tale
Narrate an epic that in rhythm and sway,
Quell the evil of hate, lies and greed,
And live through the storm to fight another day.
The worst of it all is that here, in the future someday
None will remember the fire and bile
That spewed forth in the words that you write,
And feel the pain of the nails, in your palms and feet,
For all that you have written shall be forgotten, all in vain.

PONDER THE ROAD TO TOMORROW

My dear time
Pause a moment,
Admire all that is, and purge the broken,
To glance upon the floral mirth.
Look away from the blood seeping through the earth,
To ponder the road of tomorrow,
Of joy and unity that never has been,
Not your history of struggle and sorrow?

My dear time,
Pause a moment,
Reflect on the wounds of this embattled being,
Battling with will to power, blasphemy and sin,
Peek at his colours of good and virtue,
And ponder the road to a tomorrow.
Gardens of love, of laughs and of youth,
And no graves, no grounds, muddied in tears.

My dear time,
Pause a moment,
Look over the struggle, strife and war torn horizon,
Tally the duels lost and won,
Be for a moment, mesmerized by the totem that stood the test,
And ponder the road to tomorrow.
Of royalty in simplicity and inspiration of the tiny,
Not of lofty grandeur, of greed and power.

FREE AT LONG LAST

The colour of my skin,
The creed of my birth,
The place of my right,
Will, no more, my name shall be.
Free at long last shall I be.

The road I walked,
The words I talked,
The skin I wore,
Will, no more, my fame shall be.
Free at long last shall I see.

The halo I bowed to,
The law I'm avowed to,
The tattered roof, to live under, I built,
Will decide, no more, what my fate will be.
Free at long last will I breathe.

The flaw of my fate's design,
The preaching of my faith,
The script of scriptures, handed down,
Will determine, no more, my tomorrow.
Free at long last I will go.

The threads of my past,
The truths, and lies of my fathers,
The meanderings of a legacy not my own,
Will, no more, the fabric of my life, weave.
Free at long last I shall glow.

The fodder of my choice,
The broken walls of my abode,
The hues of my humble farm,
Will, no more, the brushstrokes of my being be.
Free at long last shall I live.

The land that I plough,
The forest fruits I scavenge,
The stock that I breed,
Will, no more, the rule of my judgement be.
Free at long last will I be.

LIGHT UP THE SKY

Rest your weary mind, beaten through the battles of the day,
For a moment forget the loss of time, in pursuit of pay,
Let's forget today that tomorrow we may all pass away,
And celebrate, let's light up the sky.

Bury deep all your sorrows, and pain,
For a fleeting blink, dream away the pursuit of gain,
Let's forget that we never shall fly,
And celebrate, let's light up the sky.

Flick away the brine of lost love, and the pinch pain of lies,
For a passing while, shed the burns of goodbyes,
Let's forget all the desperations, that made you sigh,
And celebrate, let's light up the sky.

Who shall, who shall not, be not there,
May live strong in thy heart, a day and forever,
Let's wash our mourning away, as the moment draws nigh,
When we celebrate, and light up the sky.

THEN THERE IS BLACK

There comes a time,
When the taste of wine is bitter and salty,
And the smell of spring blends with the scents of decay.
When the new seems as withered as the old,
And devoid of shine, the colours of money or gold,
And nothing seems here to stay.

There comes a time then,
When all around is scarred the same,
Needy and wanting, greedy and vain.
When beauty is rare,
And the need to be has waned
Faded seems the will to be awake.

There comes a moment after,
When all is hazy and grey,
Darkness spreads slow, across night and day.
When the breath is laboured by the burdens of past,
No hurt then, will ever trigger pain,
When no words will come, no thoughts left to say.

Then there is black, lightless and bleak,
No meaning or worth, beyond,
And everything done and taken, seems void and senseless.
When all the glory of the battles past,
And all the praise penned, dried and aged,
Are reduced to banter, meaningless.

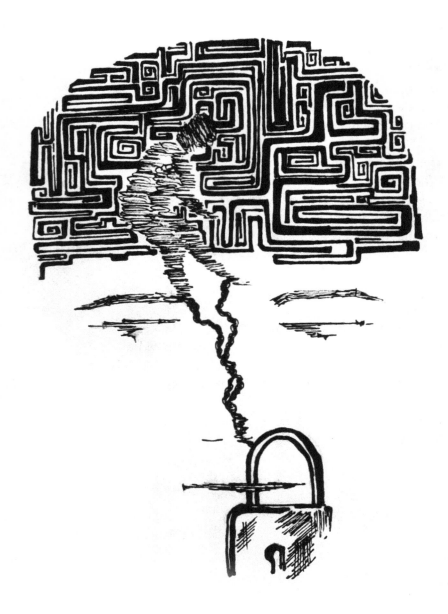

LOCKED IN

I am locked in
Away from the noise of the million sounds that filled up my every day
And, away from you.

I am locked in
Far from the distraction of a thousand moving men
And, away from her.

I am locked in
Distant from the endless barren fields that stretch on to nowhere
And, away from him.

I am locked in
Miles and miles from the cloudy horizons hiding away the morning
sun
And, away from them.

I am locked in
From the man that had once been me,
And, away from myself.

BY YOU

I was a boy - made a man by fate
I was a man - aged rough by destiny
I was old - beaten ill by luck
I was sick – to be struck dead by you.

I was a bud - bloomed before time by winds
I was a flower - weathered early by light
I was dried - parched by heat
Parched I hung – to be severed dead by you.

I was green earth - trampled by the wheels,
I was flourishing in bloom - ravished by thirst
I was empty - fattened by greed
I was dying – to be terminated by you.

AND NOW...

'Twas a dream meant to last a lifetime,
A menagerie of clouds to float eternally,
Through the skies.

And it rained and washed away,
The dream, the cloud,
Now it's baren blue sky.

'Twas a bloom never meant to fade,
A harvest of abundance, forever,
To fill the endless fields.

And the weather blew away,
The blessings of never ending plenty,
Now is endless grey.

'Twas a tune never meant to die,
A song everlasting, ever new,
To play on for life,

A thunder, a scream, a broken groove,
Broke the rhythm, mutilated the cadence,
And now, forever, piercing silence it lies.

THE TREASURE LOST

Oh! How the miracle unfurls!
The miracle of this unexplored cave,
Past every twist and curve, with fluttering nerves,
I reach out, within, the unfolding depth.

Oh! The call of the sweet dampness, of the ancient dark!
It beckons me, down the initial steep,
Through ancient cascades and pitches deep,
Through a mysterious maze of dry valleys and wet.

"To the treasure!", my heart and mind in chorus, cheer.
Breathless, I heave and sigh past the narrow hollows,
To the hallowed chambers, sought by men, by saints and kings,
Over the ages in conquest of youth, and the life it springs.

"There it is!", every muscle, bone and nerve,
Cry out in unison at the sight of the end,
Something adorns the mantle of treasure, shrouded in strange lights and mist,
I rush on ahead, with renewed strength, "Oh there it is!"

Just within reach, "one last push", and I will be there.
And feel the touch of God, and revel in its warmth,
"Oh stop!" I see it slipping away, into the dark caverns again,
Just a few steps short and I've been felled plain.

Lifeless I lie along the battlegrounds,
Of so many fights to win the coveted crown,
"Someday again," my broken heart sighs,
"We shall rise to conquer the sceptre of the divine."

HERE

Everyone said I should not go there,
Everyone said it may not be wise,
But the heart does do what the mind knows wrong,
And history has led me here.

Everyone said it's not the right path,
Everyone told me to go another way,
But the heart does follow the path of the heart,
And that path has led to this day.

My God said not to say the words,
My faith told me to say a prayer,
But the heart does feel what the mind denies,
And said words are forever here.

SO MANY

So many times
I have tried so hard
But never a word of kindness thus
Has been bestowed with no expectations
Of return.

So many nights
I have toiled under the stars
But never a look of love thus
Has been glanced with no peripheral demand
Of labour.

So many lives
I have lived and died
But never a blessing of trust, thus
Has been granted with no suffix
Of blind faith.

ALL GONE

I see you standing alone by the alleyway,
Still,
So many high tides have struck and passed,
As proud and unabashed as on the day,
That day, I sailed away, last.

I see the blue eyes betwixt dark and long lashes,
Still,
Looking through my bones and muscles,
The mischief long gone, burnt to ashes,
No spark, just a faded glare unfurls.
Now without affection, what was with passion blind,
No hint of love that once, the subject of, was I,
Only tales of a storm ravaged acrid mind,
All memories, dead, of the wild spring.

What chant of the high seas, will bring back to me,
The love I left ashore, as I sailed to sea?

AND

Just today I was distracted by a thought,
Warm,
Wet,
Fragrant.

Last night I had a vivid dream,
Violent,
Fast,
Fiery.

I think I hear a sound,
Quivering,
Whimpering,
Faint.

I think I am being haunted,
Dark,
Pink,
And -

ANYTHING GOES

A strange small animal and a swarm of exotic ants,
Fruits of trees that, in the cities, are scant,
A pinkish-grey fish in a trickle that flows,
In the great forest, when the deepest hunger strikes,
Anything goes.

Burning in fire or poached in the daylight,
Peeled layer by layer or in one wholesome filling bite
Salty, sweet or sour, spicy or pungent flavours,
Out in the unknown, when that which needs quenching strikes,
Anything goes.

Intertwined creepers or standing tall and thick,
From the roots to the stalk, to the leaves hanging free,
Licking, nibbling, chewing, swallowing, silently, or with an ostensions
flourish,
Away from known elements, when the desire to devour strikes,
Anything goes.

Skimming from the surface or digging in deep,
A stagnated wet marsh or an abundant & bountiful stream,
There is so much choice, and yet so little power to choose,
When away from home, and the most ancient cravings arise,
Anything goes.

UNREAL

Who we are,
Who we want to be,
Who we can get to be,
Is all mental alchemy.

Who you are to me,
Who you want to be to me,
Who you will ever be to me,
Is all fallacy.

What anything means,
What anything is meant to be,
What anything can mean to me,
Is all grand make-belief.

What I see,
What I am meant to see,
What you meant us to see,
Is all illusory.

The path now, ahead of me,
The path that was meant to be,
The path that will set me free,
Is all the same, an elaborate fantasy.

The bigger picture, of life,
The deeper meaning of living,
The higher reason to be,
Is but an unreal reverie.

WITHOUT PAIN

Take away the sunlight from the day,
Rob the green off from a flower garden,
A journey without direction or end,
Is going through life, without pain.

Deprive the earth the changing seasons,
Imagine a sea shore sans it's waves,
Music that will, in a single tone, play,
Is going through life, without pain.

Take the consciousness from the brain,
And strip the soul away from life,
A whiff of perfume is but alchemy in the air,
Is going through life, without pain.

I HAVE ALWAYS ONLY SEEN A FLOWER

I have always only seen a flower in the colours it spreads around,
I have always seen the sky as blue and grey, sunshine and cloud,
I measured the distance on my journey by the distance from my past,
Here in the shade I am, here be therefore, I must.

I see a child smile, it fills up my heart with glee,
Every time the rain washes through my garden, I run out to see,
I measured my stature and size, by my height from the ground,
Here therefore I live my life, in the shadow of the mount.

When a tune touches my heart, I sing along in mirth,
The scent of spice and brew, makes me feel hunger and thirst,
I measured my success and loss by the feeling of your love and warmth,
Here I breathe therefore, the darkened air, down on earth.

ANTHOLOGY OF FAITH

Lying in a pool of blood, tonight,
He beckons his God for a sign.

A sign that his prayers and prostrations,
Had not all been in vain.

Sign of heaven's promises and treats,
Were real, not the priest's deceits.

Deceit that led him away from his kin,
And away from his land and hull.

And, drew him to raise a sword,
In the name of a false God.

A God who now has abandoned him,
As has his hopes and dreams.

But the fading dream of her loving lips,
Lingers on, fading out and in.

Fading out are the lights of heavens,
The heavens that never were seen.

As he mumbles the only verses ever heard,
A poem of the great aura of God.

His heart yearns to sing, of an earthen home,
Fields of harvest, green and gold.

And sing of her hair, and her bosom fair,
But the words don't rhyme, no lines do pair.

The warmth of love that through his veins, had flowed,
Have dried up, and bled out, and gone up in smoke.

He lies there cold and withered from war,
A broken will and a broken sword.

The scavenging heathen picking loot,
"Die curs, die and rot" they sing aloud.

Howling, screaming, the chants of win,
"Long live the King," on and on they sing.

"Praise the lord, praise the faith,
"Praise the angels and the wraith."

He listens, quiet, every breath shallow and hard,
Amid battered armours and the rotting dead.

No rhymes, no cadence, no tunes and no reason,
Words spew from deep within.

Words of the seasons, promises and prayers,
Stories of love and sagas of hate.

He hath no hope anymore, of fortune or fame,
Revealing that which is buried deep, within.

His head and body, heart and mind,
Weaker with every word, every breath.

As he rambles on, barely a wisp of wind,
He gives to the skies, his Anthology of Faith.

TO A LONELY END

I've had to let you drown,
In a puddle not of your making,
For I had to keep me above ground,
In the battle of being the last man to be.

And now I am standing alone,
All friends passed by, all feelings deadened,
So little meaning, so much gone,
Life, through time, hastened.

A path beyond, there are forests dark,
Of evil spirits and gangrenous souls,
Monotonous howling and the occasional bark,
And the haunting songs of aging owls.

To the East is a cloudy sky,
With the beckoning of a ravaging storm,
Waves hammering a desolate sea side,
No place for a king or gnome.

To the West, the sun has set,
The aura fading fast,
To a starless, moonless, endless night,
Freezing cold, meant for no wanderlust.

Lying ahead is a rocky slope,
Stony and barren slopes masking many a dead,
Alas up I must climb to my tomb,
To be buried and forgotten, a shallow grave.

IT

It, rises every morning when my eyes blink open,
It, flows and ebbs as I battle through the day,
Fills with life when I sing and pray,
Burns, faint but sure, when my eyes to rest I lay.

It, I see in the eyes of those I love
It, I feel in the hearts of the racing souls around,
In the nascent bloom and profound green,
In the shapeless clouds, you, I have seen.

It glows, is there in the church down the street,
It glows, flows endless in the sermons of the priest,
Rises high in the din in the endless market streets,
And glows in the twilight streaks

It, is always there, always has been, always will,
It, walking away, will be there still,
In my thoughts, in my wake, in my happy dream,
In the road to destiny, through the snow, the blush and the summer heat.

It, shall a cohort be, as far and deep as I go,
It, shall be, through trials and tribulations, through deluge and storm,
Over the exultant peaks, under the dreary moat,
Through the deadly swamps, and through fields of gold.

FORGOTTEN AND BURIED

3 AM she started to scream
3:05 I woke up from my dream,
She continued to scream and cry for help,

3:15 I pulled the blanket over myself,
3:20 she quietened to a rhythmic sobbing,
Relieved, I gradually turned back to sleep.

7 AM, Monday morning, noisy wheels and sirens,
7:30, uniforms came knocking,
I heard some noise, middle of the night, I said,

8:30 AM, everyone had sulked to another Monday,
9:00, the alleys were quiet and barren again,
My neighbour was violated and murdered that day.

9 PM Monday, the news came alive with debate and dissent,
9:30, the opposition was outraged, in a heart wrenching comment,
Dinner was takeout and leftovers from yesterday,

10:30 PM, an old movie, and a magazine, and my bed,
Midnight, tossing and turning, irritable and awake,
A bitter taste, must be something I ate.

HERE NOW, AND GONE

Here in a breath, and in a trice, gone,
Like a splint spark to damp timber,
A whiff of wet smoke, and no flares beyond.

Like a lightening flash across a cloudless sky,
An unannounced streak of silent light,
A white fast fading line at the back of my eye.

A stray rock rolling down the slope,
A threatening and loud, clatter and boom,
And then silence and quiet follow.

Like a loud bang that makes you jump on your seat,
A stray, poorly timed, knock on a base drum,
Amidst a sad tune, out of place, out of beat.

It splashes on suddenly, and passes on away,
Like a feather of cool dry wind,
On a windless, sultry and hot summer day.

SHE

She must know,
She must weigh in,
She must understand.
She will love,
She will smother,
She will mete out punishment.

She is plain,
She is, at heart, complex
She is sun and cloudy sky.
She is teary,
She is, beneath, a pillar upright,
She is always there, always a watchful eye.

She has questions,
She has the answers,
She has worked out the world's ways.
She has soft tunes,
She has harsh beats,
She has the chorus, bridge and verse.

She can kill,
She can move a mountain,
She can be a breeze, blizzard and hailstorm.
She can be peace,
She can be the God of war,
She can grow and, in a breath, burn.

IF

If, for one day, you could wish
And your every wish could be all true.

Would you want for pots of gold,
Or yearn be for the ethereal,
Or yearn to taste, a taste of the bare and real?

Would thy heart opt for fear, or love,
Or, would thy mind search for faith,
Or would the soul avenge thy ancient tears.

Would the mind search for the meaning of life,
Or unearth the language of a stone aged wraith,
Or unravel the twists of these winding trails?

Would you fight the battle for the one true God,
Or climb a path to the anointed divine,
Or fight, and bleed, for an obscure cause?

Would your day be your legacy eternal,
Or just another day of endless struggle,
Another morning and night, to your burial?

YOU ASKED ME HOW I AM

You asked me how I am,
I am doing just fine.

The bricks of my moral foundation,
Have been split, cemented and split apart again.
And everything I thought was fair and true,
Has been taken away from my faith.
My bedrock view of the world
Has been perverted and empty laid.
You asked me how I am doing.
Doing just fine I said.

I have lost the war for truth,
To an army accoutred with myth.
Loaded to the hilt with pagan beliefs,
Girded with weapons of allegiance to the beast.
I am, now, drained of my lifeblood,
Bleeding freely from my vein.
You asked me how be my health.
Doing just fine I said.

Monuments of atrocity, you have built,
On the battle loot of my brethren, fallen,
To the prejudiced devotee, to the raging bigot
Who ravaged this, once a pristine valley of vines.
I am deafened to injustice,
And blinded by this, your dogmatic divine.
You asked me how I felt.
Feeling just fine, I said.

My heroes have all passed on by,
To the sphere of the distorted doctrine,
That preaches the value of life,
Be eroded freely by greed of faith.
I am lying here smeared,
In colours of shame and sin.
You asked me how I am.
I must and therefore I am,
I am just fine, I said

I WILL NEVER SAY

Every morning when you wanted devotion,
I only wanted the sun in my face,
I never said.

Every time you decreed, he was princelier than me,
I only wanted a simple life,
I never said.

Every other time you wanted a scholar for me to be,
I struggled through each day,
I never said.

Every time your rage, a spate of disgrace on me,
I breathed it all in,
I never said.

Every sunrise and sundown, your virtue forced its way,
In pain, I walked your way,
I never said.

Every noon and night, I fought for your fight,
I bled for your fate,
I never said.

When you never looked my path, but with judgment in your eyes,
My dreams always were, a thorn to pluck away,
You said your trodden path, was the key to my every day,
When I wanted only, my claim to my life,
You robbed me of my strength, to bear the fruits, of my own fate,
I never said.

Today when you rest all your sorrow and misery on me,
I will quietly walk away,
I'll never say.

BRUSH STROKES

[I]
Is this a curse?
This lack of muse and potent verse?
Or just a darkened blot in time,
That will lead me back to my rhyme.

[II]
How many times I have been in love, ask you?
A question for he who, in the light of enlightenment, bask,
I found a reason to live, dance and sing, but once,
And an anthology of music, a lifetime to last.

[III]
Be this the new form of insanity?
To go around, and round,
To discover the path, virtuous straight,
Never then to be found.

[IV]
I yearn to be the one,
The one with free will to be,
The one with precious freedom to speak,
The one with rare independence to act,
The one with reach to be healed,
The one to live and die, free.

[V]
A golden cube
A diamond encrusted crest,
Hand carved ornate mythological tales.
Gates of heaven, and
Embers of hell, sculpted on slates,
The royal grandeur of an epic, tells.

An eon of war,
Of good and evil deeds,
The birth, life and ascension, of God and Demon.
Victory on display,
Pride of a people, in time arrested,
Affirmed by court and country, by pious and heathen.

[VI]
What be this madness?
Over bricks, and an idol,
And who said what, and what not.
Please, my people, my countrymen, my kin,
Fall not so low that the light stops showing,
The path out of the hole.

[VII]
An eye for an eye, can't a foundation for faith be,
An open heart, or tolerant mind is not a dark and blinding veil,
The coronation and grandeur, blinds us from the residing evil,
An epic of a shallow villain, a poor and vacuous story does make.

Proportion of my church of prayer, can't a measure of my devotion be,
For the malevolent scoundrel shall prove then, the most ardent devotee,
Peace and love, encrusted in the heart, is thy true measures of fealty,
The tree giving shade to the tender and the feller, is not turning the other cheek.

The reverberation of my prayer, is not the measure of its credence,
The brightness of my flames, meaningless glow over a lonely existence,
My code of virtue need be not announced in to evidence,
My fairy of right, and my dark angel of wrong, must be of own shoulders, burdens.

[VIII]
When the ache in your heart makes your eyes smile,
And the cacophony of the world is music to the ear,
When you walk a mile more than your feet can bear,
Know that it is true love you have touched there.

When cloudy skies make you happy as sunshine,
And drenched and soaked, you feel lighter than air,
When, of the irrational belief, you begin to care,
Know that it is true love you have touched there.

When the mountain overcome feels like a stroll,
And, the leagues of cold ocean does not wear,
When bitter cold bites no more, fire doesn't burn,
Know that it is true love you have touched there.

When the saddest song makes you happy,
And, the harshest sermon feels light to bear,
When you lose your way back home among streets you know,
Know that it is true love you have touched there.

When the longest battles and carnage feel strangely just,
And the shortest wait feels like a never-ending year,
When you want now more yet will settle for no less,
Know that it is true love you have touched there.